Other titles in the series:
The Crazy World of Aerobics (Bill Stott)
The Crazy World of Cats (Bill Stott)
The Crazy World of Cricket (Bill Stott)
The Crazy World of Gardening (Bill Stott)
The Crazy World of Golf (Mike Scott)
The Crazy World of the Greens (Barry Knowles)
The Crazy World of the Handyman (Roland Fiddy)
The Crazy World of Hospitals (Bill Stott)
The Crazy World of Housework (Bill Stott)
The Crazy World of Learning to Drive (Bill Stott)
The Crazy World of Love (Roland Fiddy)
The Crazy World of Marriage (Bill Stott)
The Crazy World of the Office (Bill Stott)
The Crazy World of Photography (Bill Stott)
The Crazy World of Sailing (Peter Rigby)
The Crazy World of Sex (David Pye)

This paperback edition published simultaneously in 1992 by Exley
Publications Ltd. in Great Britain, and Exley Giftbooks in the USA.
First hardback edition published in Great Britain in 1988 by Exley
Publications Ltd.

Copyright © Bill Stott, 1988
Reprinted 1993. Third and fourth printings 1993

ISBN 1-85015-358-2

Printed in Spain by Grafo S.A., Bilbao.

Exley Publications Ltd, 16 Chalk Hill, Watford, Herts WD1 4BN,
United Kingdom.
Exley Giftbooks, 359 East Main Street, Suite 3D, Mount Kisco,
NY 10549, USA.

the CRAZY world of RUGBY

Cartoons by
Bill Stott

≣EXLEY

MT. KISCO, NEW YORK • WATFORD, UK

"I saw that – you swallowed my whistle!"

"School rugby? It's done wonders for his character but not a lot for his teeth."

"Not releasing the ball ref? He <u>can't</u> release the ball."

"And leave their No.3 alone. He once got sent off for eating a spectator's dog."

"We need a new physio – he's using air freshener on my knee again ..."

"_How_ many seasons since you played?"

"The ball! I caught the ball!"

"*This is a sending-off offence, you know!*"

"O.K. lightnin' release the ball!"

"Just think – we go through this every week because
some silly little public schoolboy picked up the
ball and ran with it!"

"Yes I did collapse the scrum. So would you if their No. 3 kept asking you what aftershave you used."

"Actually, he was hoping you'd send him off then he could go home and watch the international ..."

"Oh, ha, ha, very funny ..."

"Wait."

"I think I lost a lens."

"French referees usually have some quirky ideas about rule interpretation."

"Then Daddy shouted 'Up lads and at 'em', bopped their No.3 in the eye and got sent off."

"Lovely run – beautiful dummy, but you can't score tries with their number seven's boot ..."

"You can't have your ball back till you say sorry for pushing me over."

"Did I stick my thumb in his eye? Certainly not..."

"... it was my finger."

"That? – It's the ref's car. . . ."

"That? That's our star player – he gets too excited if we let him out too early ..."

"You know the old rugby maxim about no matter how rough and vindictive the game might have been, it's always forgotten in the bar?"

"Well?"

"Well, it's not true."

"Aaaagh! I'm stamping on my own hand!"

"So I said to her – you wouldn't love me if I didn't play rugby on Sunday and roll home full of beer would you – she said yes!"

"*It works out at 26 sandwiches each, but my Terry likes his all at once …*"

Rule 528: *"A good big 'un always beats..."*

"...a good little 'un."

"Stiff-arm tackle Malcolm when his mum's watching at your peril ..."

"No.3 – stop telling jokes!"

"Great kick – now do it with the ball."

"You think they <u>play</u> badly? Wait till you hear them sing!"

"*There he was – way offside, so I naturally looked around for you – to draw your attention to the infringement. You were nowhere to be seen.*"

"So I floored him."

"For heaven's sake – what now?"

"Let's find the bung and let him down."

"He once had a county trial. They found him guilty."

"Go on Ref, don't call it off. Our forwards hate it too firm..."

"We can't find your teeth, but here are a few nobody claimed last week."

"*What do you mean, I'll look better with all my teeth in? This is all there are!*"

"Teeth, glasses, hairpiece – sure you've taken everything off?"

"Chauvinist? Don't be silly – shut up and give us a kiss …"

"Don't worry about there being anything wasted, our No.5 will clear up for you ..."

"I can't find the first aid box anywhere, so I'll bring him round with this bucket of wa ..."

"Rugby is <u>not</u> violent. I'll belt the next bloke who says it is!"

"Great horned tortoiseshell or not – kick the ball!"

"You can stop looking for a doctor in the crowd – it was his own who did it!"

"I warned you about talking back to this referee, didn't I?"

"You're a very lucky man – not yet 20 and already invited to the President's brawl …"

"There are uncompromising players, dirty players, and Trevor."

"Lousy kicker, but an absolute whizz at building the little mud towers the ball goes on."

"O.K. – I've got him ..."

"*After a rugby match, there are no winners and losers, just drunks.*"

"When you're 6'6" and 300lbs, no one minds if you wear a shower cap."

"Did you win, then?"

"Two-and-a-half minutes … that's some Will Carling!"

"Sorry, I didn't recognize you without your gumshield."

"He was hoping to turn out for the vets this week, but he fell off a bar stool."

"Go on – he called you a rude name – then what?"

"Hang on ref – be right with you …"

"Well played – whoever you are!"

"*Get that dog into a shirt and a pair of shorts and we're in with a chance.*"

"Nice try – no ball – but nice try!"

"You're quite right, I did play rugby. How did you guess?"

"I hate rugby, but I _love_ rolling in mud."

There! He'll have to stop – Rule 198, subsection (B), paragraph 4 'The corner flag shall at no time be used for anything other than marking a corner'!"

"He's just like his car – big, flashy and nowhere near as fast as he looks."

"Actually, I have it on good authority that he doesn't have a boy at the school. He just likes shouting at young people."

"And in the fifth team, youth and maturity are united by one common factor
– total lack of ability!"

"It's not my fault. Can I help having an overprotective mother?"

Books in the "Victim's Guide" series

($4.99 £2.99 paperback)

Award winning cartoonist Roland Fiddy sees the funny side to life's phobias, nightmares and catastrophes.

The Victim's Guide to the Dentist
The Victim's Guide to the Doctor
The Victim's Guide to Middle Age

Books in the "Fanatics" series

($4.99 £2.99 paperback)

The **Fanatic's Guides** are perfect presents for everyone with a hobby that has got out of hand. Eighty pages of hilarious black and white cartoons by Roland Fiddy

The Fanatic's Guide to the Bed
The Fanatic's Guide to Cats
The Fanatic's Guide to Computers
The Fanatic's Guide to Dads
The Fanatic's Guide to Diets
The Fanatic's Guide to Dogs
The Fanatic's Guide to Husbands
The Fanatic's Guide to Money
The Fanatic's Guide to Sex
The Fanatic's Guide to Skiing

Books in the "Mini Joke Book" series

($6.99 £3.99 hardback)

These attractive 64 page mini joke books are illustrated throughout by Bill Stott.

A Binge of Diet jokes
A Bouquet of Wedding Jokes

A Feast of After Dinner Jokes
A Knockout of Sports Jokes
A Portfolio of Business Jokes
A Round of Golf Jokes
A Romp of Naughty Jokes
A Spread of Over-40s Jokes
A Tankful of Motoring Jokes

Books in the "Crazy World" series

($4.99 £2.99 paperback)

The Crazy World of Cats (Bill Stott)
The Crazy World of Cricket (Bill Stott)
The Crazy World of Gardening (Bill Stott)
The Crazy World of Golf (Mike Scott)
The Crazy World of the Greens (Barry Knowles)
The Crazy World of The Handyman (Roland Fiddy)
The Crazy World of Hospitals (Bill Stott)
The Crazy World of Housework (Bill Stott)
The Crazy World of Love (Roland Fiddy)
The Crazy World of Marriage (Bill Stott)
The Crazy World of The Office (Bill Stott)
The Crazy World of Photography (Bill Stott)
The Crazy World of Rugby (Bill Stott)
The Crazy World of Sailing (Peter Rigby)
The Crazy World of Sex (David Pye)

Great Britain: Order these super books from your local bookseller or from Exley Publications Ltd, 16 Chalk Hill, Watford, Herts WD1 4BN. (Please send £1.30 to cover post and packaging on 1 book, £2.60 on 2 or more books.)